The Magic o

Renuka Gavrani

The Magic of Creative Living

Dedication

To all those *'average'* people who spent their entire lives trying to be good enough

The Magic of Creative Living

Index

Introduction

Part One: Being

Chapter 1: Learning to BE
Chapter 2: Design Your Life Mindfully This Time
Chapter 3: Practice The Art of Being
Chapter 4: Embrace the Art That You Are

Part Two: Living Creatively

Chapter 5: Should You Aspire to Be a Loser
Chapter 6: Say YES to Life
Chapter 7: Goodbye Old Friend—FEAR
Chapter 8: Creative Climate: How Our Surroundings Shape Us

Conclusion: You Are Life's Prettiest Muse

Acknowledgments
About the Author

The Magic of Creative Living

Introduction

Is creativity only for a certain '*lucky-selected*' people who are chosen by God or by a mysterious force of the Universe to create something that will be remembered by the generations to come?

If so, then, are the rest of us simply designed to live a 'normal-not-so-important life' that has nothing interesting to offer the world? Are we, the 'normal-unselected' people, not as important as the 'chosen' ones? Is creativity only entitled to writers, artists, musicians, and the like who matter more than us?

This book is an attempt to break the stereotypes attached to creativity. This book is a message to the *'normal-unselected people' written* by a woman who thought she was too dumb to even think of becoming creative. Through this book, I want to say to the world that creativity is the birthright of every person who lives under the sun. Everyone can be creative. Most importantly, everyone should be creative, not just with their work or professional lives, but also with themselves and their very *normal life.* Even if you are not in the 'creative field', you are supposed to rekindle the spark of your heart to fulfill the wishes of your soul. To live and lead your life in such a way that life is turned on by you.

If you are questioning 'But I cannot be creative, I am not that smart' or 'How will I make my life creative' or 'What does this author mean when she says "The Magic of Creative Living", allow me to take you on an exciting journey after which you would rethink about life and yourself.

When Your Belief Stands Agaisnt You:

I grew up believing that I was dumb. I watched adults around me (not my parents though) comparing me, at every chance they could get, with my cousins, siblings, and neighbor's kid just to conclude that how every other kid was better than me. It was not like I didn't try to be good but irrespective of 'how much I studied', things just wouldn't sit in my mind and despite my best efforts, my grades were lower than expected.

In fact, when I used to get those summer assignments, I was always looking to hide my face. My classmates used to come up with some really creative assignments while I couldn't. I used to scratch my head like a wild animal yet I couldn't create anything beautiful. The worst part was even when I tried to copy their assignment, I could create nothing but trash.

That was how I made a belief in my mind that I could never be creative. I was told that creativity was for intelligent people or rather for *'selective'* people. Soon enough, I concluded that creativity was not for people like me, for I was neither intelligent and definitely not the 'selected one.'

Then after college, when I started my career as a writer, I was scared to death. I thought even if I got a job as a writer, they would kick me out when they realized that I was a dumbhead with no creative ideas to offer to them. I was lucky that my first job didn't involve much creativity. I was working for a travel agency and my job was to simply write the description of all the staycations. After leaving that job, I joined another company as a copywriter which meant that I had to be ultra-creative. However, my worst fear came alive. Whenever I offered a new idea or wrote a creative headline or a tagline or the like, my boss seldom liked it. And like most bosses when she didn't like my ideas, which was most of the time, she would yell at me like I was not a breathing human who had emotions. As long as I worked for her, I lived in self-doubt - blindly accepting that she was right.

However, again just like during my childhood, no matter how hard I tried and how much I blamed myself, it didn't work. I couldn't make my boss happy. And by the end of four months, I was completely shattered. If you throw a mirror from the top of the building, it would be shattered into thousands of pieces and could never be fixed, right? I was that mirror back then. I could hardly manage to get out of my bed in the morning. Just the thought of facing my boss was like sitting in front of the devil. I hated mornings and I loved the weekends. I started living for the weekends so I could take a few breaths in peace. I left the job within four and a half months of joining.

You see when I joined my second job, I was like a little kid for whom nothing was impossible. My mind was jumping with endless possibilities of a glorious future - one day, I would become one of the best copywriters in the world. I read biographies of famous copywriters and analyzed their work, and for the first time in my entire life, I felt excited about my work and that I finally *'fit in'* here.

Somehow my imaginary world didn't align with my reality. Every time I wrote something or presented a new idea, my boss would say *'You have written this? Like this, you would never be able to make it as a writer.'*

The thing is, no matter how much you try to fly, if someone keeps pulling you down, you end up falling. No matter how big your dreams are, if someone keeps reminding you how small your potential is, you end up believing them. No matter how brightly your eyes sparkle when you think of your dreams, if someone keeps telling you that 'you are not good enough to achieve them', your spark dies and turns into the darkness of self-doubts.

Something similar happened to me. My excitement turned into self-doubts. I hated the mere thought of waking up and doing the work that I wasn't good at. I left the job, giving up on myself and my dream of becoming a copywriter. I thought I wasn't good enough for it.

Today, I am certainly not the best copywriter. But hey! I am an international best-selling author. I have written a book, *The Art of Being Alone*.

Does Life Change Magically, Then?

Don't worry. This isn't one of those typical self-help books that start with a sad storyline and end up with *'I became successful, I figured out the secret of life and if I can do it, so can you.'*

I am not interested in sharing the tips, tricks, or hacks to change your life. For, I don't know how to do that. I am here to tell all those people who were called *'dumb'* or who believe themselves to be one, that creativity is for everyone, even for people like us. I never learned writing through any course nor did I hire an editor to help me. My previous book was a result of who I am.

And with this book, I want to tell you that, to become more creative, you have to become more YOU. Creativity is about creating something unique. Something that either has not been done before or creating a better version of anything that already exists. To make that happen, you have to touch that 'uniqueness' in you that makes you different. You are unique. You are like no one else. That's a given fact. Just when you become *'different,'* you will be able to unlock the secret door to creativity.

I have divided this book into two sections. The first section will help you to BE YOU' then the second section will be about 'CREATING.'

I must give you an FYI though. If you are looking for quick fixes or sudden hacks that will help you become more creative, I am sorry this book isn't for you. You can throw it out. I cannot line up the examples of famous creative people from history and over analyze their lives just to make a list of common hacks they all applied in their work.

When I think of creativity, I think of my mind. The depth of my heart, the beauty of my thoughts, and the magic of my soul. When all this comes together, I believe, it invites creativity. I don't think you can ever become creative by applying someone else's routine, hacks, techniques, or advice in your life. **Creativity is the birth of that hidden seed in your mind that was ignored for so long. Creativity is a reflection of you and how you live. The more original you are, the more artistic your life is, and the more creative you will be, *effortlessly*.** That much I can promise.

If you are ready to take the long road, let's walk together and create a life and a *'being'* that is the muse of creativity. Shall we?

Part One: Being

Chapter 1: Learning to BE

'You are not a lost object that can be found. You are a human. You can only BE YOURSELF.'

Are we still talking about creativity? If you are wondering that, let me tell you one thing. You don't become creative by applying hacks. You become creative when you become more YOU.

The world today is obsessed with the concept of *'finding yourself',* especially Americans. They think if they try a little harder, meditate, join a new course, travel to Bali, or eat Pasta in Italy, somehow they will find themselves. They will find the person they are supposed to be originally but the world, and its constant advertisements made them something else. So let's all meditate, close our eyes, go to Bali, take trips, and read spiritual books to '*find'* ourselves.

But I have only one question. **Are you an object that is lost by its master? Are you an item that somebody hid somewhere and they cannot remember where?**

No! You are a breathing human. Someone with a mind and a will of their own. Someone who can think and create. Going to any place won't help you find yourself because you are not lost to begin with. And joining any new course by any spiritual master won't help you find your real version because **'no one can tell you WHO YOU ARE.'**

We have been constantly fed this idea that if we find our true version then we will be happy like a monk. We are taught to apply tricks and hacks to find the lost *'real us.'* But the truth is, you are not lost. You and I are just buried deep inside ourselves and the person we are becoming is a collection of what society (and now influencers) show us who we should be. We want to be creative and live a life that reflects the beauty of our hearts but we are living it as a person whom society chooses for us.

Let me explain it to you with an example. When I started my career, although I was excited about my work and had big hopes for my future, I began with a belief that *'I was not good enough'* to do anything. Why? Because that was what I was forced to believe as a child. Then when I left my job, it was engraved in my mind that I could never be creative. I didn't have the magic inside me that creative people were supposed to have. I was not the chosen one after all.

The first four to five months after I left my job, I stayed inside my mind. I kept replaying the words of my boss. I kept watching videos on how to be a good copywriter. I followed so many copywriters online who were claiming to teach copywriting with their free videos and courses. But no matter what I did, I simply couldn't figure out what I was doing wrong. I read books on creativity, watched YouTube videos, and tried listening to podcasts by artists. Then, for a brief period, I was involved with a few people with whom I had done an online course on freelancing. The four of us met online and decided to start an agency to provide copywriting and designing services. I was happy to know that 'if they have selected me, there must be something about me, right?' With that excitement, I began just to conclude once again, 'I cannot do it.'

There was another girl in our group who was also a copywriter. Anytime there was a copywriting job, she would overpower me and move ahead with her idea. I, being extremely shy and introverted, could never say anything to her. After a point of time, I was fed up so I told them I could not work with them because I was taking up a job and that I didn't think I could manage two things simultaneously. By this point, you may think, I am just a big leaver *(as Joey says in FRIENDS).* But I think there is no point in staying at a place where your opinions, ideas, and voice are neither heard nor respected.

You might think that all of this collectively might have shattered my confidence. But I went a step ahead. I GAVE UP. I gave up on my dream of becoming a copywriter. I gave up on seeing myself winning awards for writing creative ads. I gave up on the idea of success, and creativity. I had no willpower at the time to fight against my mind or self-doubts. So I officially said to myself, *'I am giving up. I cannot take this burden any longer.'*

The Magic of GIVING UP

You must have read this line thousands of times in books and on social media, *'Don't give up. You don't fail when you lose. You fail when you give up.'*

Sounds familiar?

This is exactly the kind of bullshit that makes all of us weak from the inside. We are forced to believe that if we don't complete what we started, then we are not good enough. We are forced to drag this burden until it kills us from within. Let me prove why giving up can be one of the most beautiful things in your life.

When I gave up, I didn't give up on my dreams or my hopes. I also gave up on society's way of living life or making it big in life. I gave up on the ideas that I had collected since childhood from my external environment. I gave up on everything that I had learned from online creators and courses. I gave up on the definition of *'success'* and beliefs around *'what we should be by this age.'*

I was not only mentally but physically tired. Neither my mind nor my body allowed me to continue living a life that didn't feel good. I was trying to do everything that was suggested yet, somehow I wasn't able to make it big. And I knew for a fact that I couldn't be such a big stupid. So, I GAVE UP.

I think 'There comes a time in your life when you are just so damn fed up with trying, running, and hustling that you just want to give up. You know you are behind in this race of life when everyone else is already at the finish line. But something in you calls for you, and you realize **'Wait! What if I don't want to run in this race? What if I want to walk on the other path that is peaceful and a lot more satisfying? What if I don't want to feel this heavy?'**

Mind you, I still didn't know what this 'other path' was going to be. I just knew I could not continue the one I was walking on. So I took a break from everything - not only from my job but also from the expectations that I thought people had from me. I said to myself *'I cannot chase success to prove to people that I am smart at the cost of my life.'* When I sat down to look at my life, I realized one common thing. For as long as I could remember, I accepted anything and everything that the world told me. I lived my life with that identity or tag. People said I was dumb. I believed it. People said I was ugly. I believed it. People were pursuing copywriting. I thought I should do the same. People said you should do this or that to earn money as a copywriter. I started doing it. People said I wasn't creative. I believed it. People didn't give importance to my idea. I didn't do it either.

And where did it get me? It got me back to my parent's house where I was sitting in my room, fighting against my own mind, finding it difficult to believe in my future, taking advice from online influencers regarding what I should do next, trying to wake up early, making a gratitude list, preparing a to-do list. Yet, I used to end the day with disappointment and self-accusations.

That was what called for my GIVING UP spirit.

And what happened after giving up?

When I gave up on literally everything, and I mean everything, I said to myself 'I will do what I feel should be done at this moment. I am not going to listen to anyone nor am I going to take advice from anyone. I am going to live my life as I am and do what I can.'

Soon, I started writing on a platform called Medium just to have something to focus on. I needed to know that I was doing something. When I initially started, I didn't set a goal of making it big on the platform or becoming the best writer or such blah blah. I just set the goal of writing one article every day. My first few articles sounded something like this: *'Five Books You Must Read, What Reading Does to your Brain, Five Reasons Reading Can Make You Smarter, Three Books to Read for Happiness'* and more such clichéd topics.

I wrote on such boring topics because that was the only thing I knew. I used to read a lot of books back then. Hence, automatically reading and books were the only topics that I was capable of thinking about. However, gradually, the titles of my articles started changing from *'Why you should read every day'* to *'Life is Beyond Churning Through a To-Do List, How To Create a Soft Life that Feels Like Heaven's Kiss, why I Demand to Be Quiet'* and the like.

Not only did the titles change, but what I was writing about changed too. From what I was reading or learning from books to what I was experiencing and thinking about life. In no time, my articles were flowing with such beautiful comments that I couldn't believe people were writing such wonderful messages to me. I was receiving emails every day where people, from across the world, were telling me how much they related to my articles, how their perspectives changed, or how my articles felt like a hug to them.

Now, you must be thinking *'Why are you telling this to me, Renuka? If you are done with bragging, would you come to the point?'*

I didn't tell you about my experience to brag about my growth. I am telling you my experience so you can observe THE CHANGE I want you to adopt in your life.

When I was living my life with the rules, definitions, and fear that was planted by society, I was a confused girl who couldn't figure out what was wrong with her. I had to read books on creativity and seek advice from the external world on how to be a better writer. Yet, even after doing everything, I could neither become good at my work nor could I feel satisfied with life.

But when I GAVE UP on society and started doing things that felt right to me, without any logic, and in a way that felt comfortable to me, without knowing where it would lead me to in the next five years, somehow I became the girl who started loving her life. I became creative by default and the love from my readers served as a dessert.

The Call To Give Up

Are you happy with the kind of person you are constantly trying to become? Are you happy with the kind of life you are living?

If the answer isn't an instant YES, then it's a definite NO. You may question *'How can I judge your life when I don't even know you, right?'* But I can tell you one thing with guarantee. When you live YOUR LIFE as WHO YOU TRULY ARE, something just calms inside you. The storm that we all are constantly fighting against in our minds change into eternal peace. The self-doubts turn into reassurance.

You can read as many books as you like, listen to endless podcasts, take advice online from strangers who are known as 'influencers,' and for a moment, you may feel 'you are going to get it.' For a week or two, perhaps, you will be motivated to claim the world as your dancing stage. But the external motivation will evaporate, and you will be back to where you started *'What's wrong with me?'* Or whatever your go-to self-doubt mantra is.

The only way you can become creative, achieve anything good in life, or feel peace within yourself is when you give up on the definitions of the world.

When you stop forcing yourself to constantly try to BECOME someone better. When you stop dreaming about becoming your dream version and start paying attention to your current version.

First society fed you certain definitions of everything - *happiness, success, and achievements*. Then the social media world is obsessed with making everyone believe that you have to BECOME your dream version. Someone better. Someone who wakes up before the sun, eats healthy all the time, makes a gratitude list, looks hot, makes an insane amount of money, takes countless trips to Paris, Italy, and the list just never seems to end.

But my question is **'If all of us are unique, how come our dream version looks exactly the same? And How can a stranger who doesn't know anything about our lives, our challenges, or our mental condition teach us how to become our dream versions? And How can you feel happy and confident about your life if the path was designed by someone else?'**

When I initially started writing on Medium, I was scared. I thought my words were no good and no one would want to read them. However, gradually when I wrote with a given-up spirit, I wrote from my heart about things that I cared about. Things that made me feel excited about life. I wrote about my mistakes and my observations. Apart from getting success from the external world, I felt comfortable. I felt at ease. I used to wake up excited knowing that I get to write my heart out. I felt at home with my life, my work, and my working style.

That's what happens when you give up on society and start to live your life with your rules. You start to feel comfortable. Society has made you believe that you should seek discomfort. You should adopt the habits of successful people, learn from them, follow their routines, listen to their advice, and BECOME better.

I have done it. And that kind of life only feels heavy, and disconnected.

A Life That Comes From You VS At You

You may adopt all the great habits of successful people. You may start to wake up early, eat healthy, make a gratitude list, and do all the things that research says will make you successful. You may create a life that reflects a productive-successful day. But 'that' life wouldn't come from you. Hence, you would never feel connected to your own life. You wouldn't feel calm or at peace. You wouldn't feel the *'silent confidence'* in your day-to-day choices. Because you are living a life that was advised to you. A life that looks like a reflection of a typical self-help book. *'That'* life would be coming **AT** you hence, you would always be struggling with or in life.

But when you give up and live your life as who you are, and do things at your own pace in your style, not only in your work but in your personal life as well, then you will be able to create a life that COMES from within you. Thus, you will be able to enjoy it, connect with life in a deeper sense, and feel a silent confidence knowing that you are doing what you love and only you know what makes you happy, what you are dreaming, and where you see yourself. That makes you comfortable with your life. Life starts to feel like a warm hug and the essence of it fills your lungs with love and excitement.

So let me say this very controversial opinion, you don't need to go out of your way to seek discomfort because that's what successful people do. You don't need to make life tough or challenging for yourself. **You need to find comfort in life.** You need to live life in such a way that everything you do makes you feel more comfortable, whether it's the clothes you wear, the time you wake up, the way you speak, the accent you carry, or the people you hang out with. Life doesn't have to be heavy or a challenge. You are not playing a sport. Life is meant to be lived, as you are. When you do start to live it as who you are, it starts to feel comforting. It feels sweet, soft, and joyful. It makes you lustful for living more.

That is the magic of giving up.

Chapter 2: Design Your Life Mindfully This Time

After years of encouragement from society to never give up, to keep going, to keep moving, and to keep doing more, let me teach you today, *'How to give up properly so you can allow space in your life for YOU.'*

Abandon the Old Beliefs/Definitions/Rules/Instructions/Judgements

Since childhood, we are constantly fed one thing on a loop - *become successful. Prove them wrong. Live your best life. Make money and travel the world.*

And when they taught us the worth of our lives depends on how successful we are, and we gladly accepted it as a 'fact', why didn't they teach us to question *'What does success mean to me?'* Why didn't they teach us to listen to our hearts, pay attention to our thoughts, and find guidance from within?'

Of course, they would never do that. Because if you realize you don't want what everyone wants then you wouldn't be an easy target to be fooled. You wouldn't be buying what everyone is working hard to buy. You would use your mind instead of trusting strangers on social media with your life. You would create a life that feels peaceful and content, and hence, you wouldn't be a money-making machine for those who become 'successful' because you are insecure. If you had thoughts, principles, and rules of your own, your life would be a reflection of your heart instead of a reflection of what everyone should have by your age. You wouldn't need books like these, and you would be happy in your own world doing your own thing and feeling satisfied with the life you have built for yourself.

You see **'your satisfaction is the biggest enemy of the capitalistic economy.'** Thus, you are trained to feel insecure, afraid, and confused from a young age. You are taught to have *'more'* materialistic possessions which every rich or successful person should have. Thus, your endless struggle with trying to be better, trying to have more, trying to prove yourself, trying to look successful, trying to achieve 'success' that you never defined for yourself.

I have gone through the same struggle for as long as I can remember. I tried to figure out 'What was wrong with me?' I tried to do everything that self-help books suggested. Not only did nothing help me but every time I tried applying any suggestion and it didn't work out, my self-doubts only increased. I thought maybe I was the one who wasn't good enough to ever achieve the kind of success I used to dream about.

Until I gave up and realized I never defined what success meant for me. I just assumed that success meant a lot of money and achievements as soon as possible, doing something important and big, and taking a lot of trips and wearing expensive clothes. And since I didn't have any of them then maybe I was a failure?

Back when I had started writing on Medium and was enjoying the process a lot, even though there was no money and no big titles to my name, I felt good. I just knew this fits perfectly in my heart. When I wrote about what mattered to me, it made me feel empowered like I was suddenly claiming my space in my life. Slowly but eventually, after a few months of giving up on my job, worldly expectations, and the rules of society, I realized that success was being able to write about what spoke to me, not letting any kind of greed influence me, and waking up with peace of mind. It might sound a little dramatic but I said it to myself, 'If I can write my heart out, and feel peace in my day-to-day life, have a good book in one hand and tea in another in the evening then those will be the most successful days for me.'

Somehow the girl who was scared 'to not become successful' went from fearing to enjoying life. The girl who never knew what she wanted to the woman who is happier and confident with her life.

When did that happen?

When I decided to give up on society's rules, definitions, expectations, beliefs, and instructions. When I realized I didn't want the success that came from the death of my soul. I didn't want the happiness that I thought was waiting for me at the end of the struggle period. When I realized I could make my own definition of success and I didn't have to become someone better to build a life that felt good to me, not ONE FINAL DAY but EVERY SINGLE DAY.

My advice to you, therefore is, GIVE UP on the definition of society and decline the rulebook that you have been following to date.

How To Give Up

A. Make Life Light:

It's easy for me to write this book and ask you to abandon everything that you have learned to date. But, doing it will be challenging for you and if not done rightly can make you feel more overwhelmed than ever.

Hence, before starting off with a bust of motivation, take your time and sit with yourself without hurrying. Ask yourself what are some of the things you do every single day in your life that feel heavy and bring self-doubts into your life. What are the things you think you are working towards but you didn't consciously choose for yourself? Is it your work? Is it a relationship? Is it trying to be a perfect daughter or partner or human that's making you feel heavier? Is there any belief or self-accusation that you carry around? Sit with yourself and figure out what's stopping you from being you. What is something you are trying to chase that you, maybe, never wanted in the first place? Ask yourself '*Is it my real dream that I am working towards? Does it make me happy? Does it feel good? Do I want my life to be like this forever? Am I becoming someone I approve of? Am I doing something because I like it or because someone recommended I should do it to be successful?'*

You have lived your entire life following the instructions of society and trying to achieve what you thought you wanted. This time, if you really want to give yourself a chance, don't be in a hurry. Don't let me or anyone tell you what you should or shouldn't be doing. Turn to yourself. Learn to identify the source of your problem. And then begin with the change, one thing at a time.

For example: In my case, I was so tired of following the footsteps of people who had *'made it'* big in life. People who knew the formula for success. So, I thought if I just did what they recommended then I could become successful like them as well. When I couldn't go on any longer, the first thing I gave up on was this toxic definition of success. I cannot tell you how light and relaxed I felt the moment I set myself free from the cage of society's definition of success. I felt that now I could do what I liked. Now I could BE myself and do what I love in a way that felt good to me.

In my case, my biggest burden was the connection between 'self-worth and success.' Every time, I thought of doing something else, I heard a whisper in my ears 'But what if it doesn't make you successful? What if you cannot prove your worth to the world?' That fear led me to keep dragging my life and keep working toward a career I was never happy with.

However, giving up on this definition of success made me feel lighter and relaxed. I didn't have to try anymore to BECOME someone better all the time. There was no audience whom I needed to prove wrong. Just me, my life, and my choices that I wanted to pay attention to. I realized I was the one who was going to live this life until I die and for God's sake, I couldn't feel this heavy any longer. Thus, I took the first step of giving up. First my job, then the beliefs and definitions that made me feel heavy, and after that the instruction and the rules that made me believe there was only one definite way to success.

So I say this to you once again.

Set Yourself FREE

Set yourself FREE. Don't let the world's toxic definition of anything cage you in your own life. Don't let anyone ever tell you what you can or cannot do. Don't let yourself believe that there is only one path to success. Don't believe in what feels heavy to your heart. Don't live a life that drowns you in self-doubts and accusations. In a world where giving up is considered a crime, choose to GIVE UP. You don't have to continue doing anything that didn't originate from your heart. If waking up early doesn't make you happy, don't do it. Stay up late and be a night owl if that's when you feel more creative. If you don't like matcha, don't drink it just to fit in. If your career doesn't satisfy you, explore other paths.

B. Strive With Satisfaction:

We are constantly told by the society to want more. More success. More achievements. More medals to hang on the wall. More money to show off. More beauty to impress the world. More work to prove the worth of your time. More responsibilities to prove that you can doit all.

But who is being happy with this kind of more?

Today when I make more than what I thought was ever possible for me, I don't think I sit down to eat the money that's in my bank account or shop every day to look like a model or introduce myself as *'Hi I am Renuka, best-selling author of, 'The Art of Being Alone.'*

The time from when I gave up to now feeling the best I have ever felt in life (for the past three years), I don't think money or my achievements have played any role in the level of my happiness or peace.

Though, the past three years have been purely magical for me. In these past three years, I learned to sit alone with myself to define what makes me happy, to claim what feels good to me, to understand myself, and to design a life that comes from me.

I have never been greedier in my entire life than I have been in these past three years. But greedy not for money or success or achievements. Greedy for different kinds of more that apparently was never taught to us.

I started to seek more joy, more self-satisfaction, more laughter, more love, more ways to enjoy life, more books to read, more exploring my inner depth, more saying YES to the hobbies and habits I enjoyed as a kid, more saying NO to things that were heavier to carry, more saying NO to anything/anyone who didn't bring peace into my life, more calmness, more simplicity, more self-talk, more sitting under the starry sky and feeling how shiny my world is, more going outside and taking long walks, more saying Yes to small things that used to make me scared, more adventure, more acknowledging my desires and trying to fulfill them, more consultation with myself, more trusting myself, more saying YES to life, more being excited for life as it comes, more being in the moment, more BEING exactly who I am, more self-forgiveness and much-much-much more enjoyment in my day-to-day life.

There are two kinds of MORE in the society. We have been running behind the kind of 'more' that society and people around us made us feel is important for a worthy life. And when you chase society's 'more', you end up having 'more imbalance, more distance from yourself, more clutter and stress, more self-doubts and criticism, more anxiety, more comparison, more dissatisfaction, more hurt, more burnout, more mental struggle and more becoming someone you are not.'

However, there is another type of 'more' that we weren't taught to look out for. This is the more that comes from you. When you choose yourself more and try to give more attention to your own inner voice rather than trusting everyone else in the world. When you realize this isn't who you choose to be and all this hard work is for something that you didn't consciously choose. When you realize you don't have to be anyone better. When you say it out loud 'I *am tired of following this path that was predetermined by the world and now I choose to take the left turn and create my own path with one step at a time.*'

In this other path, you will start finding the 'more' that leads to more joy, more love, more excitement towards your life, and more being you.

The Right MORE Turns Life Into Heaven

I had a belief that everyone in the world knew better than me. Hence, I always sought advice from other people. Always asked my friends What I should do next and when my friends weren't available to me, and I had to make my own decisions, I used to scratch my head yet would never feel confident enough to say *'Yes, this is what I want.'* Every decision I made before 2020 was based on fear, greed, self-doubt, or what I thought I wanted.

It only led to extreme burnout, mental struggle, and hatred towards life. Things changed when after giving up on the world, I started asking myself *'What do I want?'* I spent a lot of time alone - to observe my thoughts, understand my unconscious behavior and beliefs, dig deeper into my mind, and closely look at myself in silent moments to realize *'it was always the little things that made me happy.'* I started enjoying morning tea with myself and found great meaning in my words. I started doing the things that I always wanted to but never had the time for like learning a new skill, going for a long walk or just sitting around without questioning why was I wasting my time.

My days were more mundane than ever. I could spend all day by myself, doing little things that made me happy and enjoying the little pleasures of life and never getting bored or seeking company or validation from the world. Mind you, I still didn't have much money nor a clear path of *'where I saw myself in the next five years',* yet somehow I knew **this was what I wanted for the rest of my life - to feel peace in my day-to-day life and do the things that make me happy.**

Wanting my 'more' was tough because every timeI met someone—my relatives, cousins, or friends—they all had the same question for me.

'What are you up to?'
Where are you working?'

There was this one cousin who dared to say it to my face *'You wasted your parent's money in college. You should do something with your life.'*

But by that time, I had become mentally pretty strong. I knew what I wanted. I knew the world only paid attention to those who had the kind of 'more' that society deemed was compulsory for intelligent people who created something worthwhile with their lives. So, I was not mad at anyone for thinking I was a dumb girl who was wasting time. I knew it was not their fault. I was so happy and content with my own life that what others thought of me never really entered my mind. I was so addicted to my life that I only cared about my own opinion and whether I was being myself or not.

I know that when you follow your own path, you know from deep within that what you are doing is different and your choices are different. Thus, there is nothing to compare yourself against. You cannot judge yourself based on what others are able to achieve or become, because you know that is not what you want for yourself.

Self-judgments only exist when you are not being you. When you are trying to become like other people but somehow you are not able to. So you sit down to find faults within you - believing something is wrong with you. But when you are BEING YOU with full self-acceptance, there cannot be a basis for judgment. You cannot compare yourself. You can only feel peace knowing you are doing and being what you like even if that's completely different from the world's expectations of you. And somehow 'What would people think of you' stops bothering you.

See, this is what happens when you live your life as being you. Suddenly, the imaginary people in your mind who used to make you question *'What are you doing with your life?'* disappear. You stop fearing the people around you and inside your mind. You stop performing for others and start living for yourself. You no longer make choices that you think will make others proud of you but rather ask yourself *'What do I want?'* The magic of giving up on the definition of the world, not only helps you build your own belief about everything but also empowers you to trust your voice and listen to it as if it's a call from heaven.

I did it. I could have easily written articles on topics that could have helped me make more money but I stuck to my values and principles. I made a contract with myself that I would never trade my heart for money. So, I kept writing what inspired me, and gradually the girl who knew nothing ended up writing a book on loneliness - *The Art of Being Alone* which is now a best-seller. I now have the title as well as the money that the world demands all of us to have. But I can tell you, it doesn't add any peace in life. It surely makes you feel secure but **peace is a reflection of the choices you make. And if you keep making choices that come from your heart, you will end up building a life that feels peaceful and confident**.

Choosing The Right Kind of More

When you chase society's more, it leads you to feel scared and greedy VS when you chase your more, it leads you towards the choices that speak the language of your heart helping you create a life that comes from you. So define what kind of more you want and then pay attention and ask yourself, 'Where do I get more joy, more fun from?' Do more of those things. Make choices that make you feel good about life even if it feels scary. Know that the scarier it feels, the clearer it is you are following your own path. Like I did. I wrote my book even though it felt scary. I didn't know the how or afterwards. But I did because it just felt right.

If I was still chasing the *'more'* that I thought would prove everyone wrong and make me successful, probably, I would probably be hating on my boss, and myself and questioning my destiny. I would have been reading a book on how to make better decisions and listening to a podcast interview with someone who had made it big in life. But I was so fed up with advice and suggestions that I decided to give myself a chance. I began with a spirit that had given up completely on the world and my only hope was to listen to my inner voice and perhaps, this time I would get somewhere better. And well, I did. Not only in terms of money or achievement, but I am at a place in life where I feel confident with my choices and happier with the life I have built for myself. A life that's coming from me.

"There is so much beauty in choosing to live a life that comes from you rather than dealing with the life that comes AT you."

So if you think that following your kind of 'more' won't take you anywhere better, trust me, it will not only take you somewhere far more beautiful but also the journey will be so satisfying and soul-fulfilling that you won't care where you might end up being. You will just be happy knowing you are being you and you have a life that reflects the beauty of your heart. Ask yourself *'What do I want'* and don't be sad if the answer doesn't come in the blink of an eye. Just because you become conscious suddenly doesn't mean all the answers will be presented to you in a second. Know that it takes time to figure out what you like and then to gradually create a life that matches the rhythm of your heart. It requires a lot of courage to say NO to the life that you have been trained to want since childhood. It demands extreme self-awareness to create your definition of success, happiness, and peace. It won't happen overnight. It will take time for you to become conscious of your soul's desires and ditch the fear, and judgments of society. However, when it happens, you will realize that *'now you are not becoming but BEING YOURSELF.'*

Chapter 3: Practice The Art of Being

'Did you ever sit down to notice who you are being?'

I recently read *Anne of Green Gables* by Lucy Maud Montgomery and for days, I couldn't stop thinking about the character of Anne along with a few quotes and the character's thinking pattern in a few situations. Throughout the book (even after finishing it), I kept wondering 'How can someone write the exact same thing that I feel/think? How could an author born in 1874 write lines that reflect my deepest darkest insecurities and feelings that I never shared with anyone? Things that I never even accepted about myself.'

Similarly, when I was reading *Little Women* by Lousia May Alcott, I couldn't stop myself from feeling connected to Beth's character. She was the kind of person I aspire to be. Again, how could a book written decades ago have a character that reflects the person I wish to be today?

Isn't that a mystery? How you read a book or a quote and suddenly you feel understood? Or how you keep listening to that one song that somehow connects perfectly to how you feel in the moment?

How you look at an art piece and it grasps your attention like you can feel an indescribable connection with it? How you come across a random line on social media by someone who never met you and they have said the exact same thing that you needed to listen to?

There must be a reason behind it, right? How can a person who doesn't know you can create an art that connects so deeply with you as if it came from you not them?

The answer is - all the artists practice THE ART OF BEING.

We are living in a world that constantly pushes us to become someone better, someone who everyone loves, someone who looks like a dream version of, apparently, everyone's dream version, someone who is a reflection of 'successful people', someone who is smart, beautiful, disciplined, and whatnot. Someone who is quiet and mysterious but also so much fun and cool to be around. Someone who knows how to dress like a model but also looks very effortless. Someone who is dedicated towards their work but also has time for family and friends and self-care days. Someone who looks cute but never tries to get attention. Someone who knows the answer to everything yet never shows off. Someone who is healed and now works as an unpaid therapist for everyone. Someone kind and loving yet has high boundaries. Someone who is…..someone who is a lot more and always enough in every situation.

And on top of it all, as you listen on social media while becoming all this, you should also 'Be Yourself.'

Well, really how do I be myself when the real me isn't someone who I am taught a good person should be? How do I be myself when there is so much more to become?

Isn't it ironic that the same society wants us to be a lot more yet wants us to maintain our real uniqueness? When we truly are ourselves, we are neither loved nor paid attention to but always questioned and judged for our choices. When we let ourselves do what we like and then suddenly no one likes who we are being?

And of course, no one wants to be ignored or questioned, judged, or laughed at, so you go around and keep chasing the *'image'* of this *'higher/dream version'* whom everyone loves. Someone who says, does, and behaves perfectly. You make choices that don't come from your heart but rather the choices that this dream version would make. You don't live your life as who you are and what you like to do but try to do things that one day will 'pay off.' And what good does it do? It turns you into a person whom you had never chosen for yourself. A person who you thought you should be if you wanted to be successful/rich/beautiful. A person who takes you far away from what you truly are underneath all these glamorous outfits, manners, and habits. A person who doesn't feel truly like yourself. A person with whom you cannot be alone or it will remind you of the person you are constantly losing.

The one reason we still connect with books like Anne of Green Gables (or any other book you loved) is because these authors didn't write an imaginary story that came into their minds whilst sleeping. These authors, whose work is still so fresh and relatable, have written stories of their lives. They didn't come up with a creative idea to write a story that no one ever heard of. They observed their mind, studied their thinking pattern, dug deeper into their behavior, and fears, and wrote about them. They wrote about REAL human emotions and feelings which is why it still connects with people who had similar life experiences, emotions, or thoughts.

"Creativity isn't a unique idea that is sent from heaven into your mind because you are the chosen one or more talented than others. Creativity is simply a mirror of your true reflection. When you are being you, you create things that show your unique thought process or perception."

To give you an example, when I wrote *The Art of Being Alone*, I was scared that if my cousins or friends read this, they might judge me as being a loner. But when I was writing, I was confident about my perception and I knew if people read it, they would like it. I knew there were thousands of books on the same topic so why do I need to write another one? Why was I adding more opinions when so many already exist? And the answer was *because an opinion like mine didn't exist. I was not adding noise in the background. I was adding music to the lives of those who had similar experiences to mine.*

After writing my book, I didn't send it to anyone for feedback. I just knew that my book would connect with people like myself. And it did. It not only became a bestseller but most importantly, it made me realize when you let yourself BE, you connect with first yourself (your original thoughts, and feelings) and then with other people like yourself.

That's the power of practicing the art of being. Therefore, I ask you to consider for once the possibility of BEING YOURSELF in a world that is full of copy-pasted versions of what a person should be. The world has a checklist for you, at every age of your life. By twenty, you should know what you want and your purpose in life. You should be out of your parent's house and chase success like a 'successful person does.' At twenty-five, you should have an apartment in New York, live a luxurious life, have a partner who loves you, and also you must be in really good shape but also live wildly and take trips to Europe. At thirty, you should be married and start thinking about saving for the college degree of a child that you should soon have.

If you keep living your life trying to make it all happen as per the checklist of the society,

a) You would obviously need rules and instructions from society because you are following their path, and
b) You will get so tired that one day you will give up either on yourself or on life.

So the choice is really on you - **whether you want to become the dream version of everyone's dream or this time, you are ready to take a bet on** yourself and experience firsthand what's the whole fuss about 'being you.'

In case you choose the second option, I only have one suggestion for you that will help you to start your journey.

A. Stop Hiding Yourself In Your Own Darkness

"Only when you hide from yourself do you feel the need to hide from the world as well."

When I was a kid, I asked my mother very innocently, 'Mom, how come you and I don't look the same?'

My mom said, 'That's because we are different.'

I replied, 'But we are not. You have a nose, so do I. You have two eyes, one mouth, two ears, two eyebrows, and black hair, and so do I. When both of us have the same things then how come we don't look alike?'

(I feel sorry for all moms here. Kids ask such out-of-the-world questions that it could be really tough to find a logical answer and satisfy them. But then again, kids aren't polluted by the world yet…)

My mom answered, 'Honey, even though we all have similar things on our faces, we look different because what we have inside our hearts is different. You see, the beauty of one's heart shines on their face.'

I didn't understand a word my mother said. But I guess, I do understand it now.

We all grow up in a similar world that teaches us the same things over and over again until we accept its definitions and rulebook as a one-way guide to win in life. But if we make our own choices that come from our hearts, only then the beauty of our individuality can be seen in our lives as well.

But that doesn't happen in reality, does it? In fact, the majority of us spend our lives secretly hating ourselves, trying to find a perfect corner to hide our true personality somewhere deep inside our minds so we can show the person who is accepted in our surroundings. I have seen people doing that and I have observed myself being that person.

How?

When I was a teenager, I wasn't the 'cool' one. I never knew what to say to anyone. I didn't know how to interact with people. And when my cousins or friends talked about anything interesting, I couldn't add anything to it. I was neither funny nor the pretty one. So I created a belief that I am not interesting enough to hold people's attention. Or I am simply not cool enough to be a part of a better group.

Hence, I started being different. When I saw my school friends were talking about that new 'English' song, I started listening to English songs too even when I couldn't understand a word from them just so I could sing the lyrics along with my friends. When I saw everyone using abusive language in college, I started saying the same word too even when it was far from what I wanted to use my tongue for. When I heard my friends gossiping about someone, I never opposed them, rather I went along with them.

Do you see how, one step at a time, one word, one action at a time, we start to hide our true selves? It doesn't happen in big-sudden ways. It starts small. Very small. So small that you may not even notice. In fact, while doing something that you don't want to be doing, you may think *'It's not a big deal. We have to network and find our tribe so we have got to blend with them.'*

But in reality, you are actually hiding your true self because deep within you are scared that if people see you the way you see yourself then they won't love you. If they could see who you truly are, they wouldn't find you cool or interesting enough. In fact, if you accept who you truly are, you will have to burn the masks that you have been wearing all this while just so you can become someone better.

The need to hide arises from within first. Only when you feel ashamed of yourself, even if that's in parts, you would want to hide yourself. You may not like how you dress so you hide yourself in the clothes that every cool person wears. You may not like your voice so you try to adopt the tone that you think is classier. You may not like where you come from so you constantly hide yourself in the manners of that society where you want to belong.

I have done that. I feel sorry for myself, for making myself believe that I had to hide so I could be seen. But when I accepted *'Well, okay I am not the cool one. I am not the interesting one. I am not the one who knows everything. I am not the funny one. I am not the one who could have every ear and eye on her when she speaks. I am the quiet one. I know about every few things but the ones that I do, I can talk passionately about them.'* That acceptance from self-FREED me. It made me feel lighter and more comfortable. It made me feel softer in my body and helped me make decisions in life based on what I truly wanted. It helped me participate in my life as who I am.

Earlier, we talked about how worldly definitions can make you feel heavy and kill your excitement towards life. But now, I urge you to question *'how you are making life heavier for yourself by trying to hide your true self. Why do you feel the need to hide any or all parts of you? Why do you feel you are 'less'?*

Question yourself. **Question the person 'who you are being' at the moment.** Observe If there is a difference in the person you become for the world VS the person you are when no one is watching. Who do you act, sound, and feel like when no one is watching?

Because even when you abandon every worldly definition, you cannot get an inch closer to satisfaction if you continue to live behind the curtains. **You need to pull your TRUE SELF back by abandoning the mask of the person you try to wear every morning.**

One exercise that might help you in identifying *'who you are being'* is - writing a letter. Take out a piece of paper, grab a pen, or just start typing on your phone. Write the heading - Questioning Self. Now write down, when you feel the heaviest in your day-to-day life. When or with whom do you feel most exhausted like you are carrying a burden and you cannot wait to get back home?

For example: When I wrote this letter (and I still do at times), I found that I feel the heaviest when I am with people around whom I feel the need to prove my worth. I try to talk a lot, maybe because I want to make sure they find me interesting. Digging deeper, and writing more such letters, I observed that there were a few sections of my life where I was different from myself and, thus, felt heavier.

Now it's your turn. Write this letter and ask yourself *'Who are you?'* You cannot practice 'The Art of Being You' if you don't even know who you are being unconsciously. How you act, think, behave, and speak out of habit or out of the need to hide.

B. Meeting GOD: Finding Internal Satisfaction

Where do you find GOD?

I always wondered, where does one find God? There are so many religions in the world and every religion is trying to prove theirs is better than the other. If God is different for everyone then where does God live? Does he live in different places as per the religious belief of the person? And what about atheists?

Tricky questions that have resulted in historical wars.

Now you must be wondering 'Why am I talking about God in a book of creative living? What does God have anything to do with?'

There is a metaphor which I believe will change how you look at yourself.

Let's understand it through a story.

A long time ago, God was upset, so his friend asked him, 'God, why are you upset?'

God replied, 'Because, I am tired of humans. They are my most beautiful creations and for them, I created all these beautiful places, flowers, beaches, mountains, skies, and whatnot but instead of enjoying any of it, they keep whining and complaining about something or the other. And guess what? No matter where I hide, in the temples, mosques, church, or anywhere else, they somehow find me and start complaining.'

His friend said, 'I know a place where you can hide. They will never go to find you there.'

God asked 'Where is that place?'

His friends replied, 'Inside a human's heart. Humans will go everywhere to find God but they will never look deep within themselves. So hide there.'

And so God hid himself in human's heart.

I know you must be wondering how it relates to this book and who you are being.

Well, this story is not in a literal sense about God. But it's rather a metaphor that teaches us that God, i.e., your real consciousness resides deep within you. That's the reason why you feel guilt when you do something wrong, no matter how well you hide from the world, you start to feel a sense of discomfort in your presence because you know what you have done. That's the reason why you feel such a disconnection within yourself when you are not being you because something deep within cannot be fooled.

God, in this story, is not the one you worship in temples, mosques, or churches. God, in this story, is that untouched part of your soul that cannot be fooled, manipulated, or polluted by the world.

In a recent interview, Viola Davis *(oh the woman she is)* said, **"There is just a place so deep inside you that is untouched by the world, untouched by even the people in your life who love you the most. And it's just yours. It's your life's force. It's your truth. And it's your job from the moment you come out of the womb to the moment you leave this earth, to honor that in everything that you do."**

That untouched place is YOUR TRUE SELF. That untouched place is YOUR HOME. That untouched place is YOUR VOICE. That untouched place in you is YOUR GOD. And you need to touch that place. You need to honor that place by worshiping it, living your life deriving the inspiration from that place so you can be truly yourself. So, you could reflect on the innocence and honesty of that untouched place. The place that is not polluted or painted in the cool colors of the world. That untouched place is the one place where you should seek validation from.

But that's where you go wrong. You go around your life like a lost human trying to find the correct way in life. Trying to find validation from society. Trying to become the replica of society that you forget to touch your own soul. *You forget who you are.* You forget to worship the God residing in you. You forget to visit that untouched part of you that is your real consciousness. That is your truth.

In my second book, *The Art of Being Alone*, I have talked about how people often go back to their toxic ex or stay with people who drag them down, knowing fully well this is not what they deserve, just because they cannot stand the thought of being alone. When they are alone, their own mind becomes their biggest enemy reminding them of all the buried secrets and thoughts, acts, and insecurities that they have tried so hard to hide. Hence, they dread being alone.

Something similar happens when you have lived your entire life running away from your truth. You fear being alone because your consciousness starts to remind you of your truth. It starts to whisper in your ears about everything that you have been ignoring.

In my case, after I left the worldly way of life behind and gave up, I had a lot of time alone. Time just to sit with me and travel to the places in my mind where I have never been. When I shared with you earlier that I could have written on anything to make money yet I chose to write on what excited me, it satisfied me. It introduced me to the Renuka I had always ignored. It made me stronger. It made me realize that I can trust myself and that trust will lead me to the kind of satisfaction I used to read about in spiritual books. In fact, I now hold the belief that *spirituality is about believing in your truth and living your life from that untouched part.*

I have lived the past few years of my life chasing my truth. I have made some of the biggest decisions in life, in my career and personal life, with no rational thinking or advice from anyone better than me or evaluating where this would take me in the next five years. But rather sitting alone, sometimes for days and hours, to ask myself *'Is this my truth? Does this satisfy me?'*

When I decided that now I wanted to focus on my career as an author, I was scared to death. I hadn't a single clue as to where I should start, what I would write about, how to publish a book, who would want to read my work, and more questions like these. Yet, I somehow felt the most calm and peaceful. I knew these questions were valid yet I felt that what I have decided is best for me. Because I felt satisfied. Because for the first time in my life, I felt a connection with my soul. I knew, during those months, that I may not have anything to prove myself or my vision but I know I will be happier with this decision than to follow a path that is more secure and acceptable by the world. I knew that people around me used to call me a loser for I had no job, no money or no way to prove 'I was making something out of my time.' Yet, that was the period, I felt the best about myself. I cannot explain the security I felt from deep within. And above all, I knew that even if it goes wrong, I could always get a job but I wouldn't be able to wake up every day living life by silencing my voice, my desires.

That's the power of acknowledging your truth. And I am telling you this so you can, after today, make decisions after consulting yourself. There are so many parameters in the world to analyze whether you made the right decision or not. So many options to choose from who you should be. So many people to take advice from.

But above all, you should keep your soul's satisfaction. If you are truly, completely satisfied with the choices you continue to make, and there is not an inch of disconnection with your soul (with your God) that means you are truly BEING YOURSELF. Spend more time with yourself, and uncover one layer of life, of yourself at a time to observe if you feel truly satisfied with your being. If there is a part of your life that makes you feel disconnected from your truth, that's where you need to make a change.

And in future, any choice you make, ask yourself '*Is that what I truly want? Does this make me satisfied? Am I being TRUTHFUL TO ME?*'

Because, honey, I promise, You can fool anyone in the world. You can hide from anyone in the world. But not from yourself. Your truth will find you. Your God will call you back.

When you live in alignment with your truth, you feel peace and satisfied with and in life even when you are completely different from others. You just know deep within you that this is perfect for you. But when you live hiding from your truth, you always feel scared, insecure, and ashamed as if people will see what you are hiding. In truth, you are afraid of what will happen if you find your true self who is hidden so well behind this mask.

Trust me, life doesn't have to be this heavy. You can free yourself from these dark emotions by honoring your truth. By chasing validation from your God (your consciousness) rather than chasing validation of the world. When you do so, you will automatically start to BE YOU. You will master *'The Art of Being.'*

Chapter 4: Embrace The Art That You Are

'You don't create art. You are THE ART of the Universe.'

If you can take only one thing from this book, let it be this.

There is a lot of great advice in the world and a lot of perfect versions that you could be. But if the choice is available, why cannot you be so you that people are moved by you? Why don't you live your life so originally that it can inspire other people to make original choices in their lives as well? Instead of feeling jealous for not having that perfect nose or figure and attaching your worth to it, why don't you feel grateful to know that no one who has a mind and heart like yours? No one can think and move in life like you do. And it's such a privilege to make choices that take you closer to yourself. Choices that shape your life into an art piece. Your thinking is your colors. Your life is your canvas. Your action is your artistic ability. Now, paint something so beautiful that you feel awe-inspiring towards the person you are being. That you wake up feeling excited because you get to be YOU.

We are no longer living in an era where you are forced to make certain choices due to lack of freedom. Irrespective of your gender, **you have the freedom to turn this life into your best work by making artistic choices that come straight from your mind and heart**. You can choose who you wish to be. You don't need anyone's guide or perfect versions for that. Use this freedom to turn yourself into an art piece. Not an artificial art that everyone just loves to gaze at. But an artistic collection of everything that your soul loves. Don't be afraid to make your own kind of choices. Don't be afraid to make mistakes. If a decision doesn't turn out as you expected, you will still be proud of yourself for trying + you will have a really cool experience to share with your grandkids. Don't be so scared by your mind and life that you end up following other's rulebooks, instead trust your inner voice so much that you are thrilled to follow it. Don't do what everyone is doing out of pressure. You are not everyone. You are You. Do what brings peace and excitement to your life, even if it's different from anyone else. Because only when you are truly being yourself, and honor your own way of living, everything that you do suddenly turn into a creative idea. Be a collection of all those things that take you closer to joy, peace, and satisfaction. Be more than just a pretty face or good grades. Be interesting and fun for yourself. Be your own piece of art.

As we are ending this section of the book, there is a life-long exercise that I want to suggest. It's up to you if you want to give it a try or not. But this is the one exercise that I have been following for the past three years. Spoiler alert: Instead of carrying a notebook, I turn my mental pieces into articles.

Be Mindful This Time:

Take a notebook and name it - *Journey to BEING*. Take this journal everywhere you go. Write everything you feel in this journal. This is your journal to find a way back to yourself and get to know yourself in a way that you fall in love with yourself. Write about the recent book you loved and why, write about a quote that touched your heart, and write why you felt the sudden touch of sadness/happiness today. Write about how you feel about things that you think only you notice, write about your small dreams and big ones, write about your fear and your strength, write about your favorite time of the year and what it makes you feel, write about your family and friends, write about your feelings and thoughts, write something you noticed about yourself however small or big. Treat this journal as a way to channel your curiosity about yourself. Things that don't seem to matter but make you Who you are. Begin with this journal as a project of taking one step towards yourself. The more you get to know yourself, the more secure you will become within yourself that nothing external will ever be able to shatter the world inside you.

You have spent the majority of your life becoming someone you are not or someone that you thought you should be. This time, if you choose to trust yourself and hope to live your life as being you, make sure you are mindful. The world is a busy place and its glamorous way can make you unconscious again. You might end up ignoring your intuitions because the world is constantly telling you what you should be and how you should live. And if you are not mindful and not checking in with yourself *'Do I want this?'*, you will end up running in this race again. Hence, practice this simple exercises for the rest of your life. The more you write in this journal/notebook, at least you will give attention to your own opinions and thoughts. That's the whole point!

Part Two: Living Creatively

Chapter 5: Aspire To Be A Loser

"Your life is your creative legacy. How you live it will define how creative you become"

I have a question. May I ask?

If I can wake up at a time I want to without rushing to be anywhere and if I can wear whatever I want without wanting to impress anyone and there is no drama in my life then does that make my life boring or simple? Is this the kind of life one should aspire to have? Because, look, nothing extraordinary is happening in my life and why would anyone want to live such a life? Also, this isn't the kind of life books and movies inspire us to live, right? There is always a touch of the extraordinary in all these great movies and books. Perhaps, that's why they are such blockbusters.

Someone is so poor that they might have to live on the street until they meet the love of their life who saves them..

Someone has a childhood trauma with toxic parents until they go to France and find a new way of life.

Some feel caged in their hometown until they go to college and have a blast with their new friends.

Someone is a poor-little-cute-angel type girl who ends up marrying a prince.

Someone who never had friends is now finally finding a huge group of besties in an unknown city.

Someone wants to be a writer but never could because of excuses and self-doubts until they found a great place and amazing people to inspire them to write and boom! they finally follow their muse.

I am sorry for such poor storytelling but take a second to observe the movies and books you have consumed till now and tell me how these movies and books start and end.

They always start with some big problem and end with a solution to it. In between, there is so much drama and unrealistic things that can never happen in reality.

The Havoc Designed to Ruin Our Mindset:

I am a huge fan of art whether it comes in the form of writing, reading, or watching movies.

Anything that reflects a piece of someone else's imagination is ART to me and I love to enjoy it.

But do you think art is art anymore? Or is it just a big business that's ruining our lives — slowly and silently?

Let me explain.

When you and I watch these kinds of movies or read books with an extraordinary plot twist, it hooks us because it has unexpected story turns that are beyond our real lives. Something that is beyond reality — hence it's entertaining.

If movies and books were exactly like our real lives, would we enjoy them?

No! We wouldn't watch it because we know how things are going to turn out.

But because it is beyond our expectations, it entertains us and because we watch/read such extraordinary things on a loop, **we have adopted a subconscious belief in our minds that — something extraordinary should happen in our lives as well — only then life is worth living otherwise life is boring and simple — and no one wants a simple life.**

This is one problem — we constantly expect our lives to change in dramatic ways so we can enjoy it.

The other problem is — pick any book/movie of recent times (I dare you) and tell me how they treat people who live a simple life.

These people are often treated as sympathetic characters — someone who has low confidence with either none or only one boring friend and lives a life with no fun. Such people are mocked in movies/books.

An adult who doesn't drink or party. Oh, what a shame! Must be boring.

Since you don't want sympathy from people or you don't want people to think that you are boring with no friends (*the weirdo*) you go to extensive lengths to try to do the things that cool students or cool people do like attending parties even when you wanted to have a pizza night with your close ones.

These two problems are interconnected to each other.

You believe a simple life is for losers. You don't want to look like a loser. You want a happening life with extraordinary turns. You go beyond your limit to live those extraordinary moments.

But in the end, no matter how hard you try or how far you go, life doesn't feel extraordinary to you, does it? In fact, in your quiet moments, you feel like your mind is eating you. You can feel the dissatisfaction and disconnection but you cannot pinpoint the reason. So you think, maybe I need a break and hang out with my friends.

The cycle continues. You live a life that was never yours. But a life that you thought you wanted to live because dude! It's extraordinary.

If you think I am being judgmental or harsh, tell me *'Why aren't people happy even after having everything they worked for? Why do people have to read books on happiness even when they are living the life that they thought could make them happy?'*

There is a gap. A silent hole.

What's your gap? And how are you trying to fill it subconsciously?

Ask yourself these questions.

If you can feel total peace with the life you are living and you think you are doing everything intentionally in your day-to-day life, I will say you are one of the most successful humans on the planet.

But if you feel even an inch of doubt that means there is a gap. And you are filling that gap subconsciously because you think that will make your life extraordinary or better.

Maybe that's why you shop a lot even if you don't really need anything new. Or you go to parties even if you feel tired and displeased afterward.

I don't know you so I cannot find an answer for you. But you CAN know YOURSELF to know what's stopping you from living a seemingly simple boring life.

Why I Aspire For A Simple and Boring Life:

I love living a simple life that people may judge as boring and mundane.

But do you know what my life does for me?

It excites me. It makes my body tickle with joy when I know I can wake up a little early to enjoy a good cup of coffee whilst reading a good book. I feel good when I am sitting on my terrace soaking in the winter sun and writing this book. I feel good when I can have another cup of tea while I spend an hour from four to five in the evening, watching that tree right outside my house and notice how it glows up as the sun goes down. I feel free when I go to bed early with my Kindle under the blanket and read a good book until I fall asleep.

Sure, there is no drama or extraordinary turns in my life. I don't live close to my friends. In fact, my friends live miles and countries away from me. I don't have a crush or a boyfriend. I don't party nor do I drink.

But I am addicted to this life. I like to do what I desire like how I am currently learning to knit even when my cousin sister said *'No one learns this old-granny thing now.'* But hey, I have built a life to please my heart not to see who is doing what and then doing the same things.

This is what my seemingly simple and boring life looks and feels like. To people, I may be a loser. But this same loser is also an author and has a life that feels good.

To tell you the truth, when I initially became more conscious of my choices and started enjoying these little pleasures of life as I always wanted, I observed that suddenly the problems disappeared from my life. Life became so quiet to me that there were moments I questioned myself, *'Am I doing enough?'*

You see the world has made us believe that if you don't have problems to fight in your life then maybe you are just sitting around and not doing enough. A couple of times this thought knocked on my door. *'If there are no problems or drama in my life then maybe I am being lazy and I should do more because these are my years to take risks and live wildly.'* I felt the fear of missing out so many times on this journey. I still question myself and wonder *'If I am doing enough because no one's life can be so peaceful and fun.'*

Why?

Because we have learned that we have to fight with/in life. Instead of teaching us how to live and love life, we are taught to fight life because that is what successful people do.

Bullshit!!

In the past three years, I have done less things. Less of those that didn't align with my true nature and made me question my worth. Less of those things that didn't come from me and were rather forced on me. Less of those wild adventures that only made me uncomfortable.

And where did it lead me? It made me love my life. Sure, it's simple with no extraordinary turns or life-changing events. It flows smoothly and I just flow along with it instead of fighting it. It's not fun, as per the standards of what a girl in her twenties should be doing, but it is made up of everything that keeps my heart younger and my mind at peace. It makes me excited to wake up not because I have a job that will change the world but because I have so many beautiful things to do that change *my* world.

If that counts as a loser, I am happy to accept myself as one. But the way I look at it, I see my recent years as nothing but a creative painting of my mind. My life is my creative project and my only goal is to be as creative as I can with all the things that feel good to me.

Should You Be a Loser Too?

"A real loser is the one who never listens to the desires of their heart."

I am not going to sit here and tell you how you should live your life. If you find yourself in this chapter and you feel there may be a gap in the way you are living, work on it.

You don't have to live a life like mine. Maybe you enjoy going to parties and casual hangouts. Maybe you are an outdoor person. Maybe you cannot sit in one place for long. Maybe late nights are your thing. Whatever it is that you want — live like that.

I am neither going to push you to live a simple life nor am I going to judge you for drinking here and there. I am going to judge you if you don't live the way you desire.

So, take this chapter as a reminder to reflect on the gaps in your life (*if any*) and work on them. Don't fill them subconsciously but build a life that feels exciting one day at a time.

Build a life that you don't fight but actually LIVE. Know that you are an artist and your life is your creative project. Make it beautiful. Make it exciting. But most of all, make it *yours*.

Chapter 6: Say YES to Life

'Creativity is a lifestyle choice'

Imagine this:

You know you have to be at your office by 10 a.m. so you set the alarm for 9 a.m. But instead of sleeping early, you scroll social media endlessly and then end up snoozing off your alarm at 9 in the morning. You wake up late, look at the time, and curse yourself for sleeping so late. You leave your bed in a hurry and rush to get ready. You wear whatever you can get your hands on, do a little makeup to avoid the questions and well it's already 9:50 a.m. You don't have the time to have breakfast but you gulp down the coffee as quickly as possible only to burn your tongue a little. You rush through the door when you realize you didn't get your charger. Cursing yourself again, you go to get it in a hurry when the invisible dining table hurts your hand. You curse it for hurting you and rush back to be at the office as soon as possible. Obviously, the taxi isn't available and something keeps coming your way. You arrive late and your boss gives you a horrible look as if muttering 'You will be fired' but you want your boss to understand how hard you tried to reach on time. You even set the alarm. You start in a bad mood and end up making a few mistakes in your work and even if not, your work feels like the biggest punishment of your life. You cannot wait to go back home and get a glass of wine to relax. But instead, when you get back home, you make whatever is easy to cook or rather left in the fridge (or order from outside yet again) then you scroll social media once again endlessly just to repeat the whole cycle all over again. You cannot wait for the weekend to arrive so you can take a breath in peace and perhaps, clean your apartment.

VS

You know you have to be at the office by 10 AM so you set the alarm for 8 AM and sleep early. You left your phone at 9 PM the night before and read a good book to end the day right or perhaps, journal a bit. You wake up the next day before the alarm hits your ears, you let yourself cuddle in the blanket for a few minutes and feel the warmth of the beautiful day that you are about to live. You get up, stretch a little, or perhaps, directly go to take a shower. You wear your favorite outfit because you want to feel your best every day. Then you make breakfast for yourself, eat it, and then make a good cup of tea or coffee whilst dancing a little here and there like you are a free bird in the sky. It's only 9 a.m. and you have enough time so you sip your coffee while picking up the book you were reading last night or just sit under the morning sun feeling the warm sunlight putting a blush on your cheeks. You feel happier than ever and as you reach the office on time, people around you ask, *'You are glowing, what's the secret? Did you win the lottery or something?'*

In response, you just smile knowing in your heart that the **secret is to choose to live life instead of dealing with it.** And you make that choice every day. You do your work with a peaceful mind and end up doing it better than anyone else and your boss is happy with your progress. You go back home, change into something comfortable, light up a few candles, and relax for a bit with a glass of wine or perhaps a cup of tea. You ask yourself *'What do I want to do next?'* And then maybe you cook for yourself while a soft music is playing in the background and you are dancing in between not being aware you are doing it or maybe you invite your partner/friend over and decide to make it a fun evening, or maybe you take a long shower and afterwards go out to dine in your favorite restaurant.

The Difference: Being Mindful of Your Intentions

Did you notice the difference between the *'WAY'* of the two lives? This is the only difference between a person who is unconscious of his/her choices. A person who always has something to complain about. A person for whom things somehow always go wrong. A person who has to read books and watch videos to find *'happiness and meaning in life'* versus a person who is awake not with eyes wide open but a mind that's present in the moment. A person who chooses to make things as creative as they are instead of waiting for life to change into a perfect fairytale. **A person whose intention is clear - to live a life that's so creatively yours that you can feel excited even towards the most mundane work. That's the difference between a non-creative and a creative person.**

You don't go out there in the world to find happiness or search for the inspiration to knock on your door and then suddenly you get that million-dollar creative idea.

You live your life in such a way that your everyday life becomes your constant source of inspiration. You realize that you don't work on the creative ideas but you make your own life so creative and yourself so authentic that anything you touch becomes creative on its own. You cannot help it. You don't go out of your way to become creative, rather you live your day-to-day with so much mindfulness that when you look back, you can see how your own life has been your best creative work to date and you want to continue working on it for as long as you are here.

Choose To Wake Up: Be Mindful

I believe creativity is not only for artists, writers, or painters. I don't think creativity means working on a unique idea that only cames into your mind. I don't think creativity means being lost in your mind and creating something extraordinary.

I believe **creativity is an act of being MINDFUL.** And being creative isn't only for certain chosen ones. Rather being creative is everyone's birthright and responsibility. **Being creative doesn't mean that certain chosen ones who are better than everyone else work on something extraordinary. Instead, being creative means living your life so mindfully that everything you do in your day-to-day life reflects your unique touch, and thought process.** It's about being present in your life so much so that *'instead of just doing things out of habit',* you ask yourself *'Do I want to do it? How do I want to do it? How can I make it better for myself? How can I enjoy it more?'*

It makes me laugh and cry, at the same time, when I look at the people doing meditation for ten minutes because a random spiritual book suggested them to do so and then they wait for their lives to become just as peaceful as a monk's life or as was promised to them. Because, darling meditation isn't about trying to sit in the same position, enact and observe your thoughts, or clear your mind. NO!

"Real meditation is about BEING AWAKE in your life. It's about walking with a conscious mind and giving yourself the gift of making mindful choices in your life. It's about allowing yourself the freedom to enjoy the little pleasures of life by adding your touch to it."

If you see a monk, they eat their food with full attention, unlike you and me who scroll social media or watch Netflix whilst eating and then wonder *'Why isn't meditation working for me?'*

Real meditation is about letting yourself participate in every act you do in your day-to-day life and enjoying it, however mundane that might be. Just like the example of two different lives we read earlier.

Therefore, **creativity is not about getting ideas. Creativity is a lifestyle choice that demands an active presence in your life.**

And I know, it's easier to write about mindfulness than living with it because, well, we have been trained to live unconsciously all our lives. Look at your life and ask yourself *'How many tasks do you do in your daily life with no attention or active participation?'*

Almost everything. I don't know you yet. I can say 90% of the actions/thoughts you have in your day are all the result of habit. Something you know you have to do so you just do it. Something you don't want to do yet you do it because **you have no mental presence in your own life let alone living it creatively.**

The question is then, *what to do?*

It's easy for me to sit here and ask you to be mindful of your daily tasks but I know firsthand how difficult it is to stay mindful of our choices. This is the reason why most people are living a *'default'* life instead of living the life they truly want (and constantly dream of).

Hence, it's better to start small than try to change your entire life all at once just because you feel inspired to do so. It's better to train yourself to become mindful of one section of your life at a time than expecting yourself to become a monk suddenly. It's better to make one habit or one part of your day more creative than trying to make everything more beautiful just to feel tired and overwhelmed. *How?*

The Magical Time

How do you wake up?

There is so much that we complain about, so many things that don't go as per our plans. YET we continue to ignore the one thing that is always in our control — the magical time.

I believe *'How you start your day will decide the functioning of your entire day.'*

For the past three years, if I had been consistent with one thing — it is to *relish my morning before the world starts demanding things from me.*

For example: I wake up late. I have tried and cursed myself to wake up at 5 am and I failed terribly. So I stopped following the guidelines and started waking up at 9 a.m. It's been like this for the last three years. After waking up, I don't rush to get out of bed. I rather cuddle in my blanket and feel the warmth of my bed and it feels so good that I cannot help but feel happy for the life I have.

Then I take a quick shower, pray, and go to make coffee. I never hurry this one thing. I enjoy making coffee and *when the aroma of fresh coffee beans fills the kitchen, I take a long breath in as if to inhale the fragrance of the beautiful I have built for myself.* Then I go to my room and have my coffee while the gentle sunlight comes from my window. I enjoy every second of this part of my day. This is the time when I feel most alive and excited.

If you see, I don't do anything extraordinary yet I feel the beauty of my life gently wrapped around me. These are the feelings that capture my heart and inspire me to write.

This has been my routine for the past three years. And it is one thing that makes me so much happier and peaceful that I won't change it for the world. To me, *my biggest achievement is waking up without hurrying or blaming myself. Having a routine which allows me to be mindful and be actively present in my life.*

Isn't that a magical choice available to you to decide how you want to wake up? Isn't that a sweet pleasure of life to start your day as you want?

If yes, why are you ignoring this one pleasure every day?

I call the morning time *'The Magical Hours'* because this is the only time frame where;

a) You haven't interacted with anyone
b) You have a relatively free mind with no to-do list or stress
c) Your mind can feel the freshness of new energy
d) You are free from the expectations of the world

In your morning time, you don't have anyone to get back to. No stress from the previous day or at least you have the choice to either start fresh or continue worrying about something that had already happened.

This is the one time of the day which allows you to BE YOU. To DO YOU. To FEEL YOUR HEART. To relish YOUR THOUGHTS/FEELINGS.

Your morning time is the first chance for you to feel your life and make it so beautiful, lively, and exciting that you look forward to waking up. Your morning time offers you the first opportunity to be mindful and to live the first few hours as who you truly are, and do whatever you like. It gives you a chance to practice being mindful, to learn to make choices, to start living your days as per the desire of your heart - doing whatever it is that you have been willing to do, in whatever way you want to. It's your time to get up and claim your life before the world demands you to do what you should have been doing.

I know, there are a lot of people in the world who don't have the freedom to just quit their jobs, like I did, and live their dream lives. Maybe you are one of those people. Maybe you have a family to support or you have other obligations. Even so, no matter how many reasons are there to hold you back from living a life that truly comes from you, *YET*, **you can choose to live at least part of your day for yourself - as who you are, doing what you like, making at least a section of your day creatively yours, designing it to your heart's desire, and being so mindful that you can feel the touch of the mysterious forces of life wrapped around you.**

So, I am asking you to GIVE YOURSELF A CHANCE TO BE MINDFUL. I am asking you to gift yourself the freedom to CHOOSE how you want to live, what you want to do, and how you want to start your day. I am asking you to **realize that your purpose in life isn't just to find a great job or take trips to Europe every year but rather to live your life as your private creative assignment. You don't have to follow the routine and guidelines of successful people but rather dance to the rhythm of your mind and heart's command. You don't have to chase the definition of worldly success but instead, chase your curiosity and do things you have been planning and dreaming or wishing to do secretly. I am asking you to WAKE UP and CHOOSE to LIVE LIFE instead of wondering *'Why isn't anything new happening in my life?'*** I am asking you to take a section of your day and make it creative. Make it about yourself. Let it reflect who you truly are and how you want to live. Start with anything small, and mold it into something you have always wished to create.

Just don't live your life melting into the shadow of your default habits and excuses that in reality no one is listening to. Let yourself live creatively. Do the same things differently and add a pinch of fun to everything you do. Adopt the hobbies that once made your heart dance. Learn to cook, paint, draw, knit, or something that you always wanted to but have been putting off for a long time. Use this time as *your secret heaven* where you can be, who you truly are and do, what you have been imagining to do. Heaven and hell, perhaps, are the places we make for ourselves on Earth based on how we choose to live. When you make efforts for yourself, when you choose peace, when you become conscious of your desires and follow the lead of your intuitions, when you learn to make yourself so comfortable in your day-to-day life that your body dances internally, when instead of complaining, you find a way to make even the most mundane-boring tasks fun by simply being aware of it + combining it with something you truly enjoy like dancing a bit while cooking, or listening to music while cleaning, like stepping out from your house in such a mood that even that cruel boss cannot upset you. Life is so much more about making things fun rather than waiting for life to make the '*fun*' happen for you. All you need is a closer look at your own mind, and the mindfulness to pay attention to your desires. You need to take a pause and show interest in yourself for once, and gift yourself the chance to actually choose your way - the creative way to live life. Maybe, you don't have a job that fulfils your soul or maybe you are still in the process of getting your dream job or college. But you cannot put your life, yourself, or your desires on hold until then. Maybe you can take a part of your day and make it interesting, challenging, fun, and beautiful by living it in a way you always wished. Maybe you could take a few hours, maybe just thirty minutes to begin with, and give yourself something to work on, something to enjoy, something that makes your soul feel satisfied whether it's sitting under the morning sun, going for an early run, enjoying morning coffee with a good book, or simply giving a chance to that *'old hobby that your child version'* used to love.

Maybe this time, you don't think of changing your entire life all at once just to fail again. But maybe, you can take a section of the day and make it magical. Maybe you can create something in your life that doesn't define your *'life's purpose'* but rather gives purpose to your day, to the hours you spend making your life magical. Maybe this time, you realize, you can have purposeful acts, hobbies, and days that truly satisfy the thirst of your soul rather than you getting upset over not having a grand

purpose in life. Maybe, just maybe, this time you choose to live.

"Creativity isn't just for people who think they want to create something extraordinary for the world so that they are remembered even long after their death and their name is printed in the history book. Creativity is for you to make your life so lively and beautiful that you look forward to living it everyday. Creativity is about designing a life that is decorated with your interests, hobbies, work, a little playfulness, and a lot more love - love that you share, and receive from things and people who make you feel alive every day."

First, learn to make your morning into THE MAGICAL HOURS, and then gradually, claim one section after another to make your entire day, MAGICAL and CREATIVE. But remember, just because you feel inspired to change your life and live creatively, your life won't change suddenly. It takes time. So **be gentle with yourself. Be curious** about your intuitions and listen to them whispering in your ears 'YOUR WAY' of living. Let yourself be mindful and make creativity a lifestyle choice.

Chapter 7: Goodbye Old Friend, FEAR

No matter which corner of the world you belong to, I am sure you must have grown up with a common question banging around you *'Where do you see yourself in the next five years?'*

Funny, isn't it? How we have never met yet somehow our fears are the same and we all are insecure about our worth based on the *'perfect plan we are supposed to have for our lives.'*

It makes me question, what if we weren't trained to fear life and instead feel excitement and curiosity towards life? What if instead of finding our value based on our *'five year ahead plan',* we could start our days with a simple question: *"What do I want to do today to make my soul happy? What can I do differently today to feel more connected to life?"*

Wouldn't that be a beautiful way to live? Of course, it would be. I can say this from my experience.

In these past three years, my life has been more than *'just'* beautiful. It's not because I make more money or I travel across the world whenever I want to. In fact, I have not traveled to the places that I thought I would once I got everything under control.

I spend most of my days at home. Yet, somehow life seems really-really thrilling.

Do you know why?

Because I changed my focus.

Since childhood, we are trained to fear LIFE. To worry about life. Think about which field to choose after high school because that will define your life. Then choose a degree because that will define your life. Then choose a job because that will define your worth. At every stage, you are being trained to FEAR life. One wrong decision and your entire life will be finished. So, we become this weird fearful creature who needs to think through everything as if we are the president of a country. In fact, if a president thinks as much as you do, maybe we would be living in a better world.

Anyway, this FEAR of life is so deep within our minds that it makes us question every little choice. Thus, we are always scared to make a choice that's uncommon in society. It's easier to follow a path where everyone is running than to choose your own where you will be alone with no one to guide you and what if you take a wrong turn?

I had lived this fear for as long as I can remember until I chose to turn this fear into excitement. Let me explain through an example.

For almost eighteen years of my life, I was under confident - not being able to say what I felt, not trusting my capabilities, and hiding myself in the corners even when I wanted to be seen.

I don't know what your *'underconfident'* stage looks like (or looked like) but to me, it was like living my life with the mind of others - constantly worrying *'What would others think of me?'* If I wear this, would I look good? If I say this, would I be considered smart? More or less, I was living a life that wasn't my own.

It's quite hard for me to explain the exact situation. But if I had to, it would be like this: *'My mind wasn't my own. My thoughts were not my own. My judgments about me were based on what people said about me. I was missing from my day-to-day life.'*

When I went to college, I worked on my confidence a lot. I put myself out there. I participated in every activity and interacted with a lot of people, and my God, I was getting proposals left and right. I wasn't afraid to speak my mind and I started believing that

'I was bold.' Truth be told, I was. Certain 'bad' people were afraid to talk to me because they knew I would reply in a way they wouldn't like.

Isn't that confidence? To say what you want and feel bold?

No, it's not. No matter what the *'YouTubers'* and *'media'* teach you, confidence isn't about being able to interact boldly with people. Confidence is not about saying what is in your mind. Real confidence is not anything that you have read/heard about on the internet.

Confidence is something different.

I must be confusing you, right? Let me get this straight then.

Something has shifted in me in the past three years. I have become loud in my own life. My day-to-day life has changed completely.

I am not afraid of making decisions that once seemed too big and risky. If I want to try something new or learn a new skill, I just jump on excitingly. In fact, every time I decide to do something new, I feel a sudden adrenaline rush and love for myself and my life.

For example; I was ten or maybe younger when my cousin sister and I got bangs together. She was looking beautiful with bangs and everyone complimented her. I, on the other hand, was looking stupid. Not because I was less beautiful than her. But because I had curly hair and my mother had no idea how to manage curls (neither did I) I was looking as stupid as you can imagine. I was made fun of for my hair more than ever.

After that incident, I was so afraid every time I got a haircut. Afraid that it might make me look stupid. This incident created a fear inside my head against trying new things. For twenty years, I was afraid to try new things on myself whether it was a haircut or applying lipstick for the first time.

But now, I am not afraid. I live loudly. If I want to do something and I truly feel excited about it, I don't stop myself. I had waist-long hair. But two years back, I chopped it off completely (bob cut). I was looking stupid for a few weeks until I got the hang of it. A few weeks back, I got bangs as well. I wanted to get bangs for a very long time but I was afraid *'What if it doesn't turn out well and I look stupid.'*

Then I thought, so what if I look stupid? It wasn't like I was a princess or a model whose every move was captured and judged. Off I went to get bangs, and I am loving it. It's so simple, isn't it?

Yet doing these random experiments in my life without feeling fear of looking or sounding stupid feels so good. I believe that's what confidence looks like. That's what saying YES to fear looks like.

When you can do whatever you desire, no matter how stupid *'that thing'* is, that's when you start to live loudly with confidence.

The other day I tried to crochet a sweater by watching a YouTube video. I wanted to do it for more than a week. But I was afraid and questioned myself, 'What if it doesn't look good and I end up wasting the material and my time?' But again, who cared? I started crocheting the sweater. I might not know how it would turn out in the end. But, I know I didn't let my wish die in my heart.

Let Go FEAR With Small Things

Self-help books and biographies are obsessed with one piece of advice - *Let go of fear. Take risks. The world is constantly selling you stories of people who took 'that big risk' and how it changed their lives.*

Back when I used to read self-help books for guidance, I used to come across this advice all the time. Dream big and take the risk. But I just didn't know how I should take risks and where to start from? This was until I stopped taking advice and started immersing myself in my life. When I decided to leave all my freelancing clients and solely focus on my writing journey (almost one and a half years back), I felt scared to death. I was constantly haunted by the thought 'What if it doesn't turn out as I had planned' and what if instead of making it as an author, I end up with nothing? But the fear didn't stop me because, by that time, I had practiced listening to my inner voice and not feeling afraid of the *'what if'* scenarios.

I didn't just become confident with my choices. I had practiced trusting my choices and saying YES to one fear at a time. I don't think you can just break free from your biggest fear after reading a really powerful book or watching a motivational video. You become confident with your choices when you practice making fearful choices in your day-to-day life. When you say YES to fear with little things.

I was scared when I decided to chop off my waist-long hair. My mom said I was being stupid and I would regret it. She loves long hair. But she still couldn't convenience me this time. I thought that I had wanted to do it for a very long time. So I was going to. Instead of wondering how I would look in short hair, why not try and see it myself? And if I didn't look good, so what? Hair grows back!

Then last year, I saw 'matcha' everywhere so I decided to order it. I was scared thinking what if I didn't like it? But then I thought why was I always negative? What if I loved it? And even if I didn't, it wouldn't end the world. It would just be a loss of $20, but at least I would know something new about my taste.

Then this year, I went to this famous pastry shop in Lucknow, India. My friend let me decide what to choose. I was going for chocolate because you could never go wrong with it. But I also wanted to try blueberry cake. My first thought was what if I didn't like it. Then, I chose blueberry cake and I loved it. I got to know something about my taste and myself.

To me, these choices weren't really small. Every time, I made a choice that I wasn't sure of, it made me more confident. It helped me say YES to my fear. It helped me in letting go of my fear with one little thing at a time.

You see, how do we fear life and our choices with such small things? Isn't it quite obvious why we don't trust ourselves and need other people to tell us *'the right way'* of life? Why do we feel the need to read books on taking risks and making the right decision in life?

If you cannot say YES to the little whisper of your inner voice, how will you say yes to your big dreams?

Like anything else, you need to practice saying YES to fear. You need to show that negative demon of your mind that you are not afraid to follow your curiosity.

The fear that was nurtured in our minds by society is not weak. Reading this one chapter wouldn't help you break free of that *'fear seeking'* mindset. But with one little fear at a time, you will eventually learn to say YES to life and curiosity.

It has happened to me to date. Every time, I want to try something new but I feel scared or my mind starts imagining all the worst *'what if'* scenarios, I take a deep breath and say to myself,

"The world doesn't burn down to ashes when you choose blueberry instead of chocolate cake."

This one line reminds me that I can experiment. You can borrow this line in case you need reminders for the future.

I can only suggest the same practice to you. If you are scared of life and you are always wondering 'what ifs', I suggest you start saying YES to fear with one little thing at a time rather than expecting to become fearless and bold and can take big risks with life because you have watched a motivational video. This life is yours. Don't be afraid of it. Don't live it with fear. Don't be afraid to mess it up. In fact, mess it up more. Mess it with things that you want to try and give your dreams and choices a chance.

We have talked a lot about giving yourself a chance but how does it begin? It doesn't begin in big ways. It begins with small things. Every little choice you make in your day-to-day life will define the person you keep becoming and the life you keep living. So live it with excitement by saying YES to fear. Try that new flavor of ice cream or go to read alone in the park. Go shopping by yourself or wear something that you have always wondered how it would look on you. Give your mind a chance. Let your mind learn that you are ready to listen to it. Say to your fear *'I will do what I want even if it's scary.'*

My Recommendation: Live Loudly

I don't know what you think confidence is. But let me suggest one thing,

LIVE LOUDLY. Don't silence your wishes just because it sounds stupid or you are not sure of the outcome.' If you want to do it, JUST DO IT.

If you want to try a new haircut, go get it. And if you look stupid afterwards, laugh at yourself. If you want to learn a new skill, go ahead, and if you cannot become the expert at it, so what? You don't have to become an expert in anything to enjoy it.

Life is so much more about listening to your inner wishes and honoring them rather than constantly worrying about the 'What if' scenarios in your head. When you try new things, you feel confident. You gain self-knowledge as well. You explore new depths of your mind.

So, Live very loudly. Don't shrink yourself too thin. Don't silence your wishes. Do some experiments with your life and on yourself. Shake it up, seriously. Just don't sit there worrying about 'What if's.' Because even if one of your decisions or experiments goes wrong, it won't burn the world.

But if it turns out right, my God, you will be so happy, excited, and in love with yourself.

Chapter 8: Creative Climate: How Our Surroundings Shape Us

I did a rather dangerous experiment on myself in November 2023. As you have already read, I am quite proud of my 'simply creative day-to-day life' which I choose to spend mindfully, trying to be aware of my everyday actions and intentions. However, I got bored. I believe that even if God hands us the key to heaven, we will get bored of that place in a few days and might find ourselves curious to just have a sneak peek of what might be happening in hell. That's the reason why people forget to realize they are living at least one of their prayers, if not all.

Anyway, when I get bored with my life, I try to shake things up, experiment, and take challenges to pull myself back to my life. I remember taking a challenge of reading seven books in seven days, not touching my phone for fifteen days, learning any new skill in thirty days, or the like. It may sound childish or unnecessary to some people. But I have found such challenges help you
a) to be mindful
b) feel excited
c) stretch your capacity
d) indulge in your life.

One such experiment I did last year was not reading books at all. Yes, I know it sounds rather the stupidest thing. However, back then, I found myself too lost in books to be doing anything else. I thought I needed a break from reading to try out something else, to see what I would do if I didn't read?

Long story short, in my free time, I found myself scrolling through social media like I was getting paid for it. I started wasting time on the kinds of videos I had never found interesting. However, the damage was done. I got addicted to social media even when I wasn't finding anything particularly interesting. It was still a good enough way to silence my mental chatter, entertain myself, or simply scroll because I had nothing else to do. In a few days, I started delaying my work, not just to scroll, but just because I didn't feel like doing my work. Next, I couldn't find anything interesting to write on. Then, I found myself complaining a lot about my current life situation. In no time, I went from being the content and calm person who started the day enjoying her morning sitting under the sunlight to an average person who was too bored, too tired, and spent her morning scrolling social media and her night, sleepless in bed cursing herself for not doing the work she was supposed to do. This eventually led me to hate the person I had become hate the life I was living. The person with unfulfilled dreams and desires that I was 'too busy or tired' for.

I couldn't understand when my experiment turned into a nightmare. But I guess, **at some point**, you get tired of your shit. You can feel the silent regret in every inch of your bone. You know you should be doing what you only dream or imagine yet somehow you cannot find the courage or will to do so. You always have the right excuse to make, which ends up making you feel hateful and disappointed in yourself. You cannot understand and question yourself 'what is wrong with me? Why don't I do what I know I should be doing, what matters to me, what I know is good for myself?' You know you are being your enemy yet you cannot stop, making it even more difficult to love yourself or love your current life. It is in situations like these when most people either find a way to distract themselves to silence their minds or spend way too much time in their mind picturing perfect scenarios to come to life so they can start living joyfully once again or worse, blame themselves until their hate starts to eat them alive.

Having experienced this firsthand, I can tell you blaming or escaping isn't the solution. My experiment, in short, taught me that *'we become what we constantly see, do, hear and focus on.'*

The reason I was able to have this beautiful love affair with my life was that I was constantly doing what I loved, whether it was through reading good books, spending alone time sitting under the star-filled sky, or learning something new, or giving my little fears a chance, thus being able to naturally find the source of creativity and joy in my life. Occasionally, when I watched YouTube, I never binged but waited for the only creator I follow to drop her video. You couldn't be a fan of everyone, do you? Thus, not only did I keep my external information and noise limited but also I actively and consciously chose where I pay attention to.

However, just this one time when I let myself go FREE, I found myself doing everything I hated just to avoid what I loved. Thus, to conclude, our fears, doubts, and insecurities all are a byproduct of our external environment. Right from the people you spend time with to people you see on the internet, everything impacts your brain. And even if you choose to follow the right people, still, you cannot be lost in 'their' world. You have to live your life and in order to do that, you have to be mindful of the time and space you allow for other people in your schedule.

My experiment can teach you that much. Just a slip is enough to create havoc in your life.

Now, I want you to ask yourself, What have you been doing with your time every day?

Do you complain about 'not having enough time to try something new' just to waste time on social media? Do you ignore your dream project to take advice from people (on the internet) on how you should achieve your goals? Do you let go of your life to see how others are living their lives? Ask yourself 'What are you doing with your life and yourself?'

If you find blaming yourself yet again, I would say, give yourself a break. Be gentle with yourself. We are living in a world that is designed to keep us away from ourselves and steal our attention with something or the other. We are being fed on a loop of the same fears and insecurities. We are being shown the same script over and over again that once you solve *'life'*, you will always be happy. It's not your fault that you are trying to find the happy ending of your life's script.

But the realization is enough to start fresh. If you find yourself in my example or feel unfulfilled with your actions, I would suggest you do what I did. Which is?

Detox and Redesign Your External Environment

The first thing I did when I was burned out three years back was unfollowing everyone who made me think I was doing less, or I was left behind or I was running late in life. Even if these people were doing just their work or sharing their success stories, I knew I couldn't get the constant reminders of my failures. I stopped watching videos on productivity or success. That was my first step towards 'listening to myself and not being distracted by the world even if the world knew better.' Not listening or watching people constantly helped me feel peaceful. It made me THINK ON MY OWN. It made me pay attention to what was left - and that was my own inner voice, opinions, and thoughts. Something I had no choice but to wonder about.

What did it do? It made me a thinker or rather an independent thinker. It made me question my choices and for the first time, find interest in my desires. It was the result of limiting my external information that I could find time to delve into my internal depths.

I did the same thing again when my little experiment turned into a disaster. I didn't touch my phone for the first fifteen days and even after that, kept a mindful watch on the time I spent on social media, who I listened to, and what I paid attention to. Doing so, I automatically found a lot of time, again, to do what I was supposed to, what I wanted to. I started writing again - about my experiment, my mistakes, and how I was building a soft life back. Surprisingly, people related and I felt excited once again for my work. I started reading again and in fact, explored different niches. I wouldn't say I don't use social media at all. I do. But I choose who I watch, listen and see. I pay attention to what I see people doing. I don't lose myself in their lives. I love watching movies and series. I do so every now and then. But again, I don't do it to escape my mind or life. I do it to enjoy life and rest my mind.

So, if it wasn't clear to you, I want you to detox your external environment. Unfollow the ones you don't know why you even started following. Take a day off just to observe and analyze the kind people you watch, hear, and see and how it's impacting your life. Ask yourself *'Do I really need to listen to all this advice on loop? Do I really need to watch people's life vlog?'* **Just 'see' what you are seeing.** Detox what's not important or what cages you back. Remove what makes you question your life. Take a break from the kind of content/people who hold you back. Not just online, detox your offline world as well. If you have a person in your life who constantly reminds you of your failures, makes you question your worth, or simply doesn't understand the kind of life you want to live, maintain your distance from them. If you have to dress or speak in a certain way because you are not accepted as being you, I suggest detoxing that person from your life. If someone is a constant source of negativity or gossip, detox that person or at least limit the space and time you allow to this person.

Because, darling, everything in your external environment will have a part to play in your internal world too. So make sure, nothing or no one can influence to become someone you consciously don't choose to be.

Redesign A Creative External Environment

Rremember just like your internal world starts to shape your external world, similarly, your external world impacts your mind and thoughts a great deal. So, instead of just dealing with your external world or going along with it to be nice or trying to find an escape through it,

CHOOSE TO DESIGN AN EXTERNAL ENVIRONMENT THAT CAN INSPIRE YOU TO LIVE MORE CREATIVELY. Follow the right people and especially follow limited people. You cannot be a fan of everyone and you cannot make your life a reflection of the internet's most clichéd advice. Your external environment should be a source of fun, joy, and real entertainment for you. It should inspire you to live more rather than take life away from you. Be mindful of who you listen to and only watch/hear/see those who ignite your soul and make you excited about life. Only let those people in your life who make you feel good about yourself, people and friends who encourage you, and make you question only your wrong behavior, not your worth. Be with people who live their lives so authentically that it silently inspires you to be more yourself as well. Don't just spend time with people who are hollow to you but you still hang out because well, you have got free time and need pictures for social media. Don't disrespect yourself or your time like that. Choose the people you surround yourself with. Choose the people you follow consciously. Choose to read the books that inspire you. Books and movies that make you realize *'Oh, life has such beautiful treasures to enjoy.'* Choose to redesign an external environment that doesn't make you depressed or anxious but rather excites you for life. **An external environment that inspires creative spirit within your soul.**

In Conclusion....

You Are Life's Prettiest Muse

They say, life is your muse or maybe you should find your *'muse'* in life. A pretty common concept in the creative field.

But I think life isn't your muse. You are the muse of your life. Life is constantly giving you chances to enjoy it. Life is seducing you with its beauty. There are trees, stars, beaches, mountains, and love and kindness to enjoy and share.

However, we are here sitting down to find a solution to a problem that either exists only in our mind or is handed to us by the world.

If you can just open your eyes, and really see, you will observe that life is not something you fight or figure out. Life is something you enjoy. You don't find the purpose of or purpose in life. You are the purpose of life. You are put here to enjoy everything. I mean everything. You are put here so you can really live.

You are not here to follow a rulebook or instructions of anyone. You are not here to become anyone else. You are made perfect and given a mind of your own so you can make your own rules and principles in life. The one who made us all, whether you call it

God or the Universe, gave you a brain with the ability to think. *If God wanted you to follow rules, he wouldn't have given you the brain, right?*

You have to understand that you neither have to live like you are a puppet of society's expectations or rules. Nor do you have to postpone fun and joy in life until you have it all figured out.

After talking about how wordly definitions cage us, how we can break free of them, and how we can build a life that excites us, I don't think I have much to say. Many people would have picked up this book thinking that this book will have straight forward answer to becoming creative or how to live a life that looks like a movie.

But I cannot give you a straightforward how-to guide. Because I don't know you. I have shared my experiences, my story, and my observations with you. Things that stopped me from living my BEST life and things that made my life a beautiful magical story that I enjoy every day.

Now it's your turn to sit down and analyze where you are heading, what you are *'becoming'* or *'being'*, who you are listening to, and who you want to be. How you are living today versus how you live from now on.

If you follow a guide given by someone else, you will build a life that came from someone else AT YOU. Hence, you will always be struggling with/in life, always needing people to tell you what's good for you.

But if you take this book as your wake-up call towards your inner voice and you **start honoring your own opinions with one thought, one desire, one action, one change at a time,** you will have a life that feels purely YOURS. A life that comes from you.

So, instead of seeking advice and suggestions all the time. Instead of chasing a vague dream version, pay attention to yourself. Treat yourself like you know it. Because you do. Believe that **you are the MUSE of life and LIFE IS WATCHING YOU.** It's waiting for you to be enthralled by it. Have a lust for it, be excited for the moments of your daily life, and make them creative. Creativity is not about applying hacks to get creative ideas. It's about having a mind and heart that's so free and full of love and excitement that creative ideas search for you. Not only what you consume mentally, but how you live your life also starts to impact your creativity. When you live in unalignment with your heart and mind and repetitively do things that you don't want to, you create a life that is not yours. Your mind and your physical body are not connected. Thus, so much mental struggle and stress. But **when you slow down and live how you want to, even if it's different from others, you invite yourself into your own life. You become CREATIVE then.**

And that kind of creativity isn't only for artists, writers, or painters. It's for everyone. *Everyone should be a creative director of their lives - turning their lives into their best work without regrets and leaving a legacy behind.*

I will finish the book now.

"If your connection with your internal voice isn't strong enough then you will be controlled by the voices of the external world."

So, my dear reader, are you ready to build your connection to your inner voice? If yes, go back to the life you truly wish to live — by being you and taking the actions that will take you to that life.

Acknowledgment

I am deeply grateful to all my readers without whose support I am nothing and my words are just black ink on a white sheet. But with you, I am an author and my words have the power to soothe an aching heart and hug a tired soul. If I could, I would hug each one of my readers for showering so much love on my first book —The Art of Being Alone. I have read every email and Instagram DM that each one of you has sent. I know I have not been able to respond to every message, but know this: I have no words to express how your experience with my book has made me feel. Thank you for all your love and support. I hope you love this book just as much.

About the Author

I have made a lot of mistakes in life. And I continue to make more. I am not a 'I know everything so do what I say and your life will be perfect' type of writer. I don't have all the answers and I am still in the process of understanding life myself. I love that I have created enough space in my life to make mistakes, mess up my life, clean up the mess, learn from my failures, and not be afraid of my own self. All I want to do is live my life by staying true to myself. Although I am a big believer of slow living yet if it comes to chasing, I would always choose to chase my truth.

I want to dedicate my life writing about my experiences, observations, and the constant love affair I have formed with life. The more I write about my observations, which I used to think are unique, the more people connect with me, saying they find it relatable. I guess, deep down, beneath this fancy mask and glorious identities (religious, country, culture), we all are the same.

My aim is to simply speak from the heart so that it connects with another heart. Apart from books, I also share everything I learn, experience, or observe as I explore this silly little life. You can find more on my instagram: renuka_gavrani

The Magic of Creative Living

Printed in Great Britain
by Amazon